What Are the US Regions?

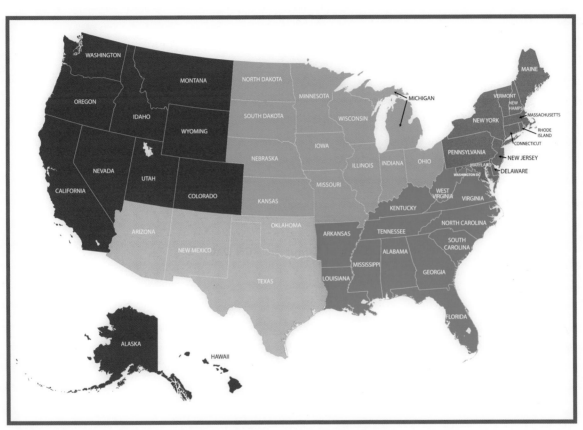

Maureen Picard Robins

Educational Media

rourkeeducationalmedia.com

Teacher Notes available at
rem4teachers.com

www.rourkeeducationalmedia.com

PHOTO CREDITS: Cover: © andipantz, subjug, Keith Binns; Title Page, Page 3, 5, 8, 11, 14, 17: © Natasa Tatarin; Page 4: © James Charron, Rob Jamieson, Jani Bryson; Page 5: © AnkNet, Richard Semik; Page 6: © Courtesy of the U.S. National Archives and Records Administration; Page 7: © wsfurlan, Mariya Bibikova; Page 8: © El Biffster at flikr, Pgiam; Page 9: © Jason Titzer; Page 10: © Evgeniy Zaharov; Page 11: © ruchos; Page 12: © Alexander Raths, Henryk Sadura, Jodi Matthews; Page 13: © Nicole S. Young; Page 14: © JasonDoiy; Page 15: © Mlenny Photography; Page 16: © eva serrabassa, li jingwang, 26ISO, Stefanie Timmermann; Page 17: © Nicholas Roemmelt; Page 18: © David Padfield; Page 19: © shotbydave; Page 20: © dma; Page 21: © Joel Johndro

Edited by: Precious McKenzie
Cover design by: Tara Raymo
Interior design by: Renee Brady

Library of Congress PCN Data

What Are the U.S. Regions? / Maureen Picard Robins
(Little World Social Studies)
ISBN 978-1-61810-145-7 (hard cover)(alk. paper)
ISBN 978-1-61810-278-2 (soft cover)
Library of Congress Control Number: 2011945872

Rourke Educational Media
Printed in the United States of America,
North Mankato, Minnesota

rourkeeducationalmedia.com

customerservice@rourkeeducationalmedia.com   •   PO Box 643328 Vero Beach, Florida 32964

A **region** of the United States is a group of states in one area of the map. The United States is made up of five regions. Let's find them on the map!

The West

The Midwest

The Northeast

The Southwest

The Southeast

The Northeast

I live in New York City. New York City is one of the largest cities in the United States.

My family and I can take the subway to the Empire State Building or the ferry to the Statue of Liberty.

Maine is the state that is the furthest north in the region. Maine has beautiful coastlines and mysterious mountains.

Maine provides the world with some of the best lobsters.

Philadelphia, Pennsylvania is where American **colonists** heard the Declaration of Independence in 1776.

IN CONGRESS, JULY 4, 1776.

The unanimous Declaration of the thirteen united States of America

The Southeast

I live in New Orleans, Louisiana. If you visit me in New Orleans, you might want to try our **Cajun** food.

Fun Fact

In Louisiana, Zydeco music blends the sounds of Cajun music with rhythm and blues. You'll hear the sound of the fiddle mixed with the accordion.

West Virginia
Virginia
Kentucky
North Carolina
Tennessee
Arkansas
South Carolina
Georgia
Alabama
Louisiana
Mississippi
Florida

The Southeast is well known for other important past times such as car racing and country music.

The Southeast is also where NASCAR began in 1948.

The Grand Ole Opry in Nashville, TN.

St. Augustine, the nation's oldest city, celebrates its Spanish heritage.

Castillo de San Marcos Fort in St. Augustine, FL.

The Midwest

The Midwest region is called America's Heartland because it grows corn, wheat, and many other foods for our nation.

The Midwest has the Great Lakes, the largest group of freshwater lakes on Earth.

The Great Lakes provide shipping routes, drinking water, and fishing spots.

I live in Chicago. Cities like Chicago, and Columbus have large universities that promote research and **technology**.

The University of Chicago.

The West

We live in California which is in the West. The West is known as the land of **cowboys**. We also have big cities and many beaches.

Fun Fact

People from all over the world visit California to see the beaches and visit Hollywood.

Computer companies and other high tech industries are in this region, too.

People call northern California Silicon Valley because of the computer companies.

Many Native Americans live in the West. They remember and celebrate the **history** of their ancestors.

Native Americans were the very first Americans.

The Southwest

I live in the Southwest. My home is in Arizona. What grows in a desert? Cactus!

Yucca

Saguaro Cactus

Prickly Pear Cactus

The Grand Canyon in Arizona, The Alamo in Texas, and Aztec Ruins National Monument in New Mexico teach us about the past.

Fun Fact

The Grand Canyon National Park is 277 miles (446 km) long, up to 18 miles (29 km) wide, and a mile (1.6 km) deep.

Texas is the second largest state.
Cattle, oil, and technology are
million dollar businesses in Texas.

Texas longhorn.

Texas is the highest producer
of oil in the United States.

America the Beautiful!

All regions in the United States are beautiful. You can find historic places to learn about the past or visit big, modern cities.

The Alamo in San Antonio, TX.

The best part of America is the hardworking, caring people who live there. Go out, explore, and meet them!

Picture Glossary

Cajun (KAY-juhn): A French person who moved from Canada to Louisiana sometime during the 1700s.

colonists (KOL-uh-nistss): People who move from far away to live in a newly settled area.

cowboys (kou-boiz): Men who often ride a horse, wear a certain type of hat and boots and herd cattle.

history (HISS-tuh-ree): The study of events that happened in the past.

region (ree-juhn): This is an area or a zone.

technology (tek-NOL-uh-jee): The use of science and engineering for practical things.

Index

Websites

www.motownmuseum.com/mtmpages/

www.maps4kids.com/

ngm.nationalgeographic.com/map/atlas

About the Author

Maureen Picard Robins writes poetry and books for kids and adults. She is an assistant principal at a New York City middle school. She lives in one of the five boroughs of New York City with her husband and daughters.

Ask The Author!

www.rem4students.com